Not a
Failed Faith

TENA MARCHAND

WESTBOW°
PRESS
A DIVISION OF THOMAS NELSON
& ZONDERVAN

Scripture quotations taken from the New American Standard Bible®, Copyright © 1960, 1962, 1963, 1968, 1971, 1972, 1973, 1975, 1977, 1995 by The Lockman Foundation. Used by permission." (www.Lockman.org)

WestBow Press books may be ordered through booksellers or by contacting:

WestBow Press
A Division of Thomas Nelson & Zondervan
1663 Liberty Drive
Bloomington, IN 47403
www.westbowpress.com
1 (866) 928-1240

Because of the dynamic nature of the Internet, any web addresses or links contained in this book may have changed since publication and may no longer be valid. The views expressed in this work are solely those of the author and do not necessarily reflect the views of the publisher, and the publisher hereby disclaims any responsibility for them.

Any people depicted in stock imagery provided by Thinkstock are models, and such images are being used for illustrative purposes only. Certain stock imagery © Thinkstock.

ISBN: 978-1-4908-1187-1 (sc)
ISBN: 978-1-4908-1186-4 (hc)
ISBN: 978-1-4908-1188-8 (e)

Library of Congress Control Number: 2013918404

Printed in the United States of America.

WestBow Press rev. date: 4/8/2014

Contents

Dedication

The children's short story in Chapter 8 is dedicated to Lacey, Kaitlyn, Eric, and Micah, my great-nieces and great–nephews, with loving appreciation for faithfully praying wholeheartedly for Nanu when she was very sick and dying. She could not have travailed in her faith all alone. She desperately needed our prayers to keep her strong. Your homemade cards that came straight from your hearts were a big source of encouragement to her. You will all be rewarded for your part in her journey when you get to Heaven. Always love Jesus with a whole heart in obedience to all His ways. I love you all so much!

Preface

I wrote this book out of compassion for children who experienced the loss of a loved one. They don't understand; and they're very vulnerable to a sense of abandonment or unwarranted guilt settling in on them. Furthermore, they may even think it's their fault. (The book was originally intended to be the short story for children in Chapter 8, but it evolved into a bit more. It ministers to people of all ages.)

My sister, Nancy, died after years of believing for a healing. I felt I knew the reason why, typed up a four-page explanation, and showed it to my sister, Sylvia. She thought it was beautiful but wished she could believe it. I then realized that the family needed time for their own closure. Meanwhile, I sought the Lord's confirmation before stepping out to share my revelation with the others when the time would be right. Sylvia soon became very concerned about how her young grand-children would be affected. They had faith for Nancy's healing, sent her weekly handmade cards of encouragement, and their church frequently prayed for Nancy. "How am I going to explain it to them?" I suggested telling them what I told her. "But how?" I hung up the phone and converted it into a children's short story within a very short time. It was not birthed from my own imagination. I just started typing straight through, never stopping to question "What next?"

It's a very sweet sad story that brings to light the beauty on the other side of death. It was Nancy's journey.

1

Background

We lost three family members in seven and a half months. The first to die was my brother-in-law, who battled lung cancer for thirteen months. By this time, one of my sisters had already gone through breast cancer for a year, then a year cancer-free, and now bone cancer for another couple of years. Their end-stage intervals overlapped. Nancy died twenty days after Walter. I remember telling people that no one should ever have to watch a family member go through death like that. Not that they should stay away, it just shouldn't happen. Unknowingly, leukemia silently blindsided a second sister by the last few weeks of Nancy's life; but she wasn't diagnosed until four weeks after Nancy's death. Despite feeling bad, Linda put off seeing a doctor until she was very sick. Commitments to her family, the home, and work consumed her time and attention. Once the doctor saw her very critical lab results, he sent her straight from his office to the hospital, dying. Filled with hope and faith

1

for her healing, we were again taking around-the-clock shifts at the side of another loved one as we witnessed her rapid decline over the next four and a half months. Linda then joined Nancy and Walter in Heaven.

I suppose I could've gotten angry with God or given up on believing Him for anything else after the final loss; but He was merciful enough to take me to a place of grace and peace that I never knew existed. It was one of those things of God that surpasses all understanding (Philippians 4:7). By no means was I spared from grief; but gratefully, my faith was left intact. It's an indispensable weapon that has no limits; and God will not leave anyone limp. When you've had answers contrary to that for which you've believed over a long period of time, don't be discouraged. Encourage yourself in Him. Disappointment will fade away. Never give up on something as precious as your trust in God.

The testing of our faith is an opportunity for it to grow as we continue to believe God for all of life's challenges. When we don't receive our desired results after we've prayed in faith, it remains a faith being built upon for all things. It was not exercised just for that one concern. Our prayers are accumulative as a reminder before God. They are all stored up in Heaven and will impact various issues throughout our journey on earth. Every time we pray over a need, our overall faith is *growing and solidifying.* Cornelius, the centurion, prayed to God continually (Acts 10:1–4). He probably prayed over many needs without seeing the answers he desired. That didn't mean that his faith was lacking or that his prayers weren't heard:

> *Now there was a certain man at Caesarea named Cornelius, a centurion of what was called the Italian cohort, (2) a devout man, and one who feared God with all his household, and gave many alms to the Jewish people, and prayed to God continually. (3) About the ninth hour of the day he clearly saw in a vision an angel of God who had just come in to him, and said to him, "Cornelius!" (4) And fixing his gaze upon him and being much alarmed, he said, "What is it, Lord?" And he said to him, "Your prayers and alms have ascended as a memorial before God."*

God took notice of Cornelius' faithfulness and was ready to move in a big way. God worked with his faith; and the same holds true for us. We may not have seen our expected answers to our fervent prayers of faith, but those prayers also ascended as a memorial before God. He cherishes every prayer of faith.

Nancy was the first to be diagnosed with cancer. It was a long journey. We were a total of nine siblings and seven spouses, nieces, nephews, great-nieces, great-nephews, and treasured friends. Many of us gave it our hearts to press in and believe for her healing. There was constant love and support from everyone.

I went from an immature, casual assumption that

Christians can be healed of any disease, to a very deep *knowing* that she *would* be. After much travail and spiritual warfare, she wasn't. The night she died, I looked up to Almighty God and whispered from the depths of my heart, "You're sovereign." I respected that, as well as His being omniscient. He sees the whole picture and acts accordingly. Ephesians 1:11 says that He works all things after the counsel of His will.

Romans 5:5 was one of the verses that anchored my faith in the healing promises. I would pray, "God, Your Word says that hope does not disappoint. We hope in You for Nancy's healing. Thank You that we will not be disappointed. Thank You for her healing." My angle on this verse was that if you don't get that for which you are hoping, you'll be disappointed. Therefore, if you weren't going to be disappointed, it was because your prayers were going to be answered as requested. I petitioned God from that viewpoint. It made sense to me. But when she died, my actual experience was different from my reasoning. The abrupt end of solid hope did not bring disappointment. More than anything, I went through a shock and disbelief that she really died. In retrospect I realized that hope didn't disappoint, because my hope was securely rooted in God Himself, and not dependent on the answer that Nancy would be healed. Not *having* to have my hope fulfilled prevented the opportunity for disappointment to emerge.

My faith shifted from belief for a healing miracle to

a hope and expectation that God would raise her from the dead. Sylvia and I sat next to each other at the burial, steadfast in that trust until the coffin was underground and covered. There are many very compelling testimonies of God's raising the dead today; and it's even happening here in America. In Hebrews 13:8, we see that Jesus never changes:

> *Jesus Christ is the same yesterday and today, yes and forever.*

Whatever miracles He did while on this earth, He continues to do; and He does them through us. In fact, in John 14:12 Jesus says:

> *"Truly, truly, I say to you, he who believes in Me, the works that I do shall he do also; and greater works than these shall he do, because I go to the Father."*

The whys and wherefores of it not manifesting may remain a mystery until we get to Heaven. However, we can keep on believing in His promises. As parents, we desire to meet the needs of our children. Of their wants and perceived needs, we deny many of their requests for various reasons; but we want them to freely express their desires and ask for our yeses as they approach different opportunities. They will eventually learn the definite nos and refrain from those petitions.

5

Any time faith is exercised, regardless of outcome, it's an integral part of its overall growth for future needs. God can use anyone who will honor Him with their faith when their heart is set to believe that His Word is true. Certain trials may require a deep search of His Word, much prayer, and sometimes fasting. Romans 12:3 says that God gives us all a measure of faith. I believe our loving Father didn't take the chance that our weak faith would falter for something as serious as eternity. He didn't leave it up to us to work up the *initial* level of faith for salvation. He graciously supplied us with the measure needed. We must exercise it from there; and He will increase it, even to levels of accomplishing the impossible.

At a time when the twelve disciples were *already* doing miracles and casting out demons (Luke 17:5), they cried out for God to increase their faith. *Earlier* in Luke 9:1–6, Jesus gave them power and authority over all the demons and anointed them to heal the sick. So that's exactly what they did as they preached the gospel: they went out into the villages, casting out demons and healing the sick everywhere. Their faith appeared to be victorious and complete for any need. That was my perception of faith at one time: you have it and it covers any challenge that comes along in life. I didn't realize I had to set my heart and mind to believe His Word in order to develop my faith. I believed it was a faith-in-general to meet any need until a never-before-encountered circumstance arose for which I needed faith, but had none. Disappointment in my lack led to discouragement and a sense of failure, but I was not abandoned to that place. The Lord gave a revelation as one of our visiting missionaries was giving testimony.

Pastors, preachers, teachers, and evangelists may never realize how the various needs of their audiences are met through their transparency on the pulpit. Such was through David Hogan, a missionary whom our church supports in Mexico. He's always been a fearless and radical warrior with a very strong, intimidating physical appearance. His armor seems to be the reflection of God's anointing that results in satan's cowering and bowing in surrender. (Note: "satan" will not be capitalized in this book.)

Brother Hogan visits our church periodically and updates us on the many exploits of his ministry. One of his amazing testimonies was of an eight-and-a-half-month pregnant woman, who died and was brought back to life— she and the baby both! He also told of his son-in-law's financing a truck that he bought (for the ministry, I believe). Brother Hogan, *who had faith to raise several people from the dead*, said that he got upset, fretting over how they would get the finances to pay for the truck. That's when I realized that you can have a tremendous amount of faith for one thing, but lack even the "little faith" needed for something of lesser impact. The great faith that he exercised for raising the dead was not effective for financial concerns. He needed to develop his faith for that specifically.

Taken from Brother Hogan's ministry site, Global Fire Ministries International:

> *David decided to go after God for His power to see the miraculous, to see "signs following" instead of only religious hypocrisy. He began to seek God to raise the dead. After four years of intense prayer and fasting he saw the first person receive life after having died, this miracle by the power of prayer to God. God has since allowed him to be present on twenty-eight different occasions to date where people of all backgrounds have been raised from the dead. In the work now there have been over four hundred people who have received this life after dying. This is one miracle of God among many that has affected the work.* (Date written unknown by me.)

As of his visit to our church in November 2012, the number is over five hundred dead raised to life.

My faith was built for healing miracles as I targeted it for my loved ones, because we were confronted with acute situations that were desperate. Other lesser needs were tolerable and accepted as a normal part of everyday life. I didn't put forth the effort to pray on those situations. The difference in faith levels directly correlated with whether or not I prayed and meditated on specific Scriptures for each problem. Brother Hogan fervently prayed and fasted for four years, focusing on raising the dead; and he achieved a very effective faith in that area. In developing our faith, what if we include four different areas of potential need? Ten? Would we have great faith for all those needs alike? Or what if we built it in general for all things? As we saw in Luke 9:1–6, Jesus instantly gave them power and authority over all the demons; and they also healed the sick. Increasing faith has tremendous potential.

The disciples had the advantage of being with Jesus for three solid years. They observed His perfection and holiness, were taught the Scriptures, and witnessed His power as many signs and wonders took place. This was their daily routine. They observed Him long enough that their faith should've been ready for the supernatural, to perform miracles in His Name. In Matthew 17:14–21, we see this expectation:

> *And when they came to the multitude, a man came up to Him, falling on his knees before Him, and saying, (15) "Lord, have mercy on my son, for he is a lunatic, and is very ill; for he often falls into the fire, and often into the water. (16) "And I brought him to Your disciples, and they could not cure him." (17) And Jesus answered and said, "O unbelieving and perverted generation, how long shall I be with you? How long shall I put up with you? Bring him here to Me." (18) And Jesus rebuked him, and the demon came out of him, and the boy was cured at once.*

What's interesting is that the people seeking the miracle thought the disciples could do it! We have to transform our minds from the mentality that the next person can, but we can't. Even though they had the advantage of Jesus Himself day in and day out, there was still the need to build their faith. They asked Jesus why they couldn't cast out the demon:

> *Then the disciples came to Jesus privately and said, "Why could we not cast it out?" (20) And He said to them, "Because of the littleness of your faith; for truly I say to you, if you have faith as a mustard seed, you shall say to this mountain, 'Move from here to there,' and it shall move; and nothing shall be impossible to you. (21) ["But this kind does not go out except by prayer and fasting."]*

He answered them with the simple truth: they were of little faith. The instinct is to wonder at that, since they were involved with Him closely for three intense years. It seems that their faith should have been soaring. How could they have missed?

Like the disciples, we are expected to have great faith also. It's been my habit to start my daily quiet times with this whisper of a prayer: "Lord, change me." I loved looking for verses to transform my behavior and attitudes; but I just casually read the accounts of the miracles, inattentive to their reality and availability to us. I was familiar with verses of the signs and wonders; but it was not a focus, and my faith was not *actively* being built with them. When my family members were diagnosed with life-threatening diseases, I started collecting every Scripture and passage that would activate, build, and maintain my faith.

Were the disciples also "just familiar" with the daily miracles of Jesus, failing to set their minds to believe that they themselves could perform them at His command? Was that part of why they were of little faith? The disciples would have good reason for bewilderment at our lack of faith: Jesus Himself, Who performs the miracles, is *in* us. In addition to that, we are promised the Holy Spirit as our Helper. When Jesus completed His ministry and was soon to depart from the earth, He left the disciples and us with these words (John 14:12–16):

> *"Truly, truly, I say to you, he who believes in Me, the works that I do shall he do also; and greater works than these shall he do; because I go to the Father. (13) "And whatever you ask in My name, that will I do, that the Father may be glorified in the Son. (14) "If you ask Me anything in My name, I will do it. (15) "If you love Me, you will keep My commandments (16) "And I will ask the Father, and He will give you another Helper, that He may be with you forever—"*

There are many catch-all verses like this one in the Bible; but it is essential to arm yourself with precise Scriptures directly aimed at defeating every attack of the enemy. During His forty days of fasting, Jesus rendered each of satan's attempts null, void, and powerless with Scriptures that opposed the very intention of those temptations.

In summary, utilize the good catch-all verses as in John 14 for all things in general, while building your faith for specifics with each promise you encounter in your quiet times. One strategy fortifies the other.

This is getting a little off the subject, but as I studied the passages in Luke mentioned a few pages earlier, I noticed a couple of things worth mentioning as encouragement to anyone battling with bitterness. It's so difficult an emotion to overcome, especially when it's progressed to the point of unforgiveness. God loves you so much, and your faith in Him will not fail you as you bring this burden to Him. Not only does He understand the depths of your pain and the difficulty to put it behind you, but He wants to set you free from it altogether.

The disciples were told to forgive every time anyone repented of an offense against them, and they realized that it took faith. In Luke 9:2 Jesus sent them out to proclaim the kingdom of God and to perform healings. The miracles happened readily. They already had a high level of faith in operation, but later in Luke 17:4–5 they asked the Lord to increase their (already great) faith:

> *"And if he sins against you seven times a day, and returns to you seven times, saying, 'I repent,' forgive him." (5) And the apostles said to the Lord, "Increase our faith!"*

To forgive an offense against them was apparently a bigger challenge to their faith than it was to move in the supernatural of healing lepers and commanding demons out. When we are hurt and wounded, satan brings pride and resistance to "soothe" our pain, with intentions of paving the way for bitterness and a stronghold of unforgiveness. But we only find ourselves miserable with the torment of it all. *Know that as long as you hate it and are sincerely trying to get past it, your heart is still tender and you are in an overcoming mode.* God is well-pleased and He will take you through. You will be set free. Don't give up and don't rely on your feelings as a guide. The words of Jesus in Mark 11:26 are sobering:

> *"But if you do not forgive, neither will your Father Who is in Heaven forgive your transgressions."*

A determined refusal is costly. satan wants to destroy and own a precious piece of your loving heart that you've given to God. The disciples knew that they needed their faith increased in order to forgive. If they had enough faith to perform miracles, then God could just as easily increase their faith to the level of truly forgiving an offender. As long as you are working on forgiveness, *no matter the ups and downs nor the feelings of it,* you're in right standing with Him. Ask Him to increase your faith. The Holy Spirit will help you get to the place that it no longer bothers you. I always saw Luke 17:4 as a command, but never realized that it took faith. Thank God that we are not left to our own efforts. Ephesians 2:8–9 says:

> *For by grace you have been saved through faith; and that not of yourselves, it is the gift of God; (9) not as a result of works, that no one should boast.*

Extending forgiveness can be a near impossible task when left to just our efforts alone; but we are no longer under the Law, where they *were* left to their own strength. God loves us so much and gives us the grace (*His very power*) needed for victory in any and every circumstance. Ask for it, receive it, and be set free. When Peter asked how many times to forgive in Matthew 18:21–22, Jesus gave the same instruction:

> *Then Peter came and said to Him, "Lord, how often shall my brother sin against me and I forgive him? Up to seven times?" (22) Jesus said to him, "I do not say to you, up to seven times, but up to seventy times seven."*

We forgive whether or not they repent. One perspective that I've experienced on this verse is that, although only *one* offense occurred over an issue that never really came to resolution, I had to bring my heart attitude back to a place of forgiveness *several times* on the *one* offense. When there's strife, the mind is a very easy target for satan. He's expert at getting us to rehash our arguments with embellishments of the imagination that trigger false scenarios resulting in MGM-size productions. The experience is relived and attitudes of unforgiveness are rekindled. He's trying to root it into your heart as a stronghold, with the purpose of searing your conscience, thereby destroying your sense of conviction and robbing you of your freedom.

Be careful of prolonging situations. One thing that I've learned to do is nip it in the bud by taking every thought captive to the obedience of Jesus as soon as it comes. Paul talks about destroying speculations and every lofty thing raised up against the knowledge of God. That's become my habit and it's very effective. For the most part, I choose not to give those thoughts any time at all. However, when the challenges are harder, I wholeheartedly take the time and effort to press in for the victory with the help of His grace. He's been faithful to bring me through to the point that it's no longer a struggle and I'm set free. Forgiving seventy times seven is living in a constant state of forgiveness, resisting satan's temptations until he flees. He's a deceiver, a master manipulator, the instigator of all strife; and he's after your soul. Fight him and him only. Ephesians 6:12 puts it in perspective:

> *For our struggle is not against flesh and blood, but against the rulers, against the powers, against the world forces of this darkness, against the spiritual forces of wickedness in the heavenly places.*

2

Nancy

Nancy died in 2005 after a four-and-a-half-year's battle with cancer. She was my youngest sister, the eighth-born of nine siblings. When there was suspicion of the disease, I promptly gave it my whole heart to believe what God's Word says about healing. According to Isaiah 53:5, I knew that we can be healed of anything:

> But He was pierced through for our transgressions,
> He was crushed for our iniquities; the chastening for
> our well-being fell upon Him, and by his scourging
> we are healed.

Just as our salvation was made possible by Jesus' death and resurrection, our healings are made possible by the stripes brutally inflicted by a whip on His back. Since He carried and suffered every single disease through the severe and brutal beating at the whipping post, we need not tolerate illness. It was a completed work two thousand years ago. In John 10:10, we see that Jesus came in opposition to satan:

> *The thief comes only to steal, and kill, and destroy;*
> *I came that they might have life, and might have it*
> *abundantly.*

satan kills, steals, and destroys. He wreaks havoc with our health, but Jesus gives us the abundant life and that includes miracles. Doctors and medicines can do amazing things, but they are limited in their ability to reverse satan's destructive forces that lead to permanent disease or death. This requires a miracle that takes place with simple faith, fervent prayer and warfare, and sometimes fasting. (Incidentally, God has anointed doctors with His power to instantly heal the sick as they pray for their patients. There are even reports of the dead being brought back to life. Search the internet for testimonies. Every kind of miracle is taking place today through preachers, and laymen as well. It can happen through you!)

At the time of Nancy's office visit for the results of her breast biopsy, I was preparing my patient's room for the birth of her baby. Nancy was on my heart all morning, and I had been silently praying for her. I was quite busy in the room when I suddenly had a definite *knowing* that her diagnosis was cancer. I had just finished putting my patient's legs up in stirrups. As I was separating the lower half of the bed, in silence the tears began to stream down my face. I looked at the clock. It was the timeframe of her appointment. Perhaps we can be in two places at one time, so to speak. On the exterior I was caught up in this family's joy of welcoming this new little life into their world, while on the inside I had a very, very sad heart that was breaking into pieces. Most of my pain was for her as she was hearing that dreadful word "cancer." I felt her loneliness at that moment and desperately wanted to spare her. I wanted to be with her, to rescue her, to somehow carry it for my precious sister.

Faced with a huge challenge that required a miracle, I discovered that my faith for healing amounted only to *assumptions* that it would be quick and easy because of the healing promise in 1 Peter 2:24. But we had to actively fight the forces of darkness and release God's healing powers into action on Nancy's body. I realized just how critical our part was in the process and engaged myself with other family members in the vigorous fight and warfare in the spiritual realm, where the real battle takes place. Gathering as many Scriptures as we could on healing, we renewed our minds to what His Word said. We spoke it, prayed it, and believed it. Our faith became indestructible and well beyond the shadow of a doubt. Poor prognoses were daily before us; but almost every time I read the Word, there were beautiful revelations of healings and miracles related to the fight-against and victory-over disease and trials of any sort. These passages were inspiring and applicable treasures that I added to my arsenal of faith Scriptures in the fight for her life.

We faced hurdle after hurdle that got bigger and bigger, but not really harder and harder to jump. Once my faith started growing in this area, it was easier and easier to develop it to the next level. Mine was a from-faith-to-faith journey. It was a very intimate and intense time with the Lord. We had many very special and precious friends who believed and fought in prayer with us. We are forever grateful to them.

My faith was initially jump-started by Nancy's. Hers was actually somewhat contagious. She had the same mindset of Matthew 21:21–22 and expected the mountains to move when she approached different trials in life:

> *And Jesus answered and said to them, "Truly I say to you, if you have faith, and do not doubt, you shall not only do what was done to the fig tree, but even if you say to this mountain, 'Be taken up and cast into the sea,' it shall happen. (22) "And all things you ask in prayer, believing, you shall receive."*

She didn't allow obstacles to stand against her faith in God, Whom she obviously loved with all of her heart. Any prayer that she prayed was like asking for the salt shaker at the dinner table—a completely normal everyday event—and the salt would be passed to the one requesting it. It was just that simple when she approached God about anything, no matter how difficult or impossible.

Nancy always taught the Bible to a variety of people: co-workers, special-needs children, geriatrics in a mobile home park, random people invited to a sister's home, etc. One of her groups was a Sunday school class of teenagers in a small town. She taught them the Word, faithfully prayed for them, encouraged them, and counseled them. She acquired a very deep concern for their welfare. Not only did she have a strong spiritual appeal with those kids, but she was also lots of fun. Nancy was very creative with various activities, while maintaining a pure example of Christ as Lord and Savior. As the teens were going into their next phase of life, they gave her a locket as a parting gift of love and appreciation. This piece of jewelry encapsulated and held the sentiments of the strong bond of love between them and Nancy. Several years later they were all coming together for a reunion. Eager to go, she searched and searched for her cherished locket. She had always worn it, but lost it sometime earlier—probably the one time she removed it from her person.

Just a few days before the reunion, lightning struck a sycamore tree in our parents' front yard. Mama wanted it removed for a long time, and they marveled at God's goodness to take it down for her. As this massive tree lay across the yard, Nancy noticed the glistening of the sunlight in a bird's nest on a very high branch. It was her necklace with the locket! She then remembered rocking one of the nieces on the front porch. As the baby drifted off to sleep, she had a firm grip on the locket. Concerned that the little one might pull on it and break it, Nancy took it off and put it on the banister, inadvertently making it accessible to a bird as she built her nest. She retrieved the necklace right in time for the reunion.

It's so easy to exclude God from some of our problems. Things happen so fast and we just don't take the time to include Him. Not Nancy. She consistently went to Him first. It was an automatic, a reflection of her oneness with Him. Far-fetched needs held no restraints for her. No matter what situation she faced, she approached God boldly for His intervention and fully expected His direct response.

When Nancy was twenty-eight, Daddy died a sudden and unexpected death. She then purposed to devote her life to Mama. After they moved into their last home, they had the living room repainted what they thought was a muted mauve color. To their surprise and distaste, it was a shocking pink. When the painters finished, they poured the remainder of the paint down a drain in the backyard. A little later, Nancy noticed from the corner of her eye and through a front window, a shocking pink trail running down the street from their home. The paint traveled through an underground drain that emptied onto the road. New-comers to the neighborhood, she was horrified and cried out to God. Within minutes the rains came in a heavy down-pour, just long enough to wash the paint away without leaving any trace of pink. The sun promptly returned, restoring the beautiful clear day that it was intended to be.

Nancy lived with a sense of loneliness, but she was so full of life and very interactive with people that it was undetectable. She and I were the only two of the sisters and brothers who never married. She would be described as the-life-of-the-party type person. She was amusing, entertaining, and had an unparalleled sense of humor, very witty. On the serious side, she was readily equipped with profound words of wisdom for any sort of dilemma. Her wisdom came from spending prolonged periods of time reading her Bible—probably much more than the average person—to get to know the Lord and to strengthen her part of the covenant with Him. Much of her learning was also through books by reputable Christian authors.

When it came to faith, hers was a faith of action. She was definitely a doer and not just a hearer of the Word. God used her tremendously in people's lives from day to day. It seems that when Nancy ministered to others, it soon created a deep bond of appreciation, love, and admiration. When I met those who knew her, I got the same response *every* time they discovered that we were sisters. Their countenance became very solemn, they focused in on my face, paused, and said, very softy and firmly, "Ohhhhh, she touched me deeply." "She made a difference in my life." "My life turned around because of her." "I will never forget her as long as I live." The remarks were consistently of this nature. She had a very influential affect on the family as well. Nancy was a great Christian role model and never drew attention to herself. Philippians 2:3–4 explicitly reflects Nancy's death to self as she allowed Jesus to live in her:

> *Do nothing from selfishness or empty conceit, but with humility of mind let each of you regard one another as more important than himself; (4) do not merely look out for your own personal interests, but also for the interests of others.*

She lived a life of self-denial and maintained a focus on others in their needs. People were her mission. She never refused anyone, no matter how tired she might have been or what the circumstances were. Inconvenience and money were no objects. She never uttered a complaint. While Nancy could not be with Jesus in Heaven, she devoted her life to serving Him with real *actions* of His love toward others.

I have witnessed her reaching out to people of all ages in their needs. She seemed to have been magnetized very compassionately toward the hurting. To watch her minister was better than any preaching. I learned much of our Father in Heaven by observing her in action. She was an indisputable example of a submitted life to God. She didn't look to herself as anything special; and she was no respecter of persons.

In her latter years, she was in ministry with special-needs children. Their mishaps with hygiene didn't matter. A draining nose or drooling mouth didn't hold her back from getting cheek to cheek with them. Wet or dirty pants were no obstacles. She took them right onto her lap and gave big hugs that communicated acceptance. Bless their little hearts, they were accustomed to being in the background, generally ignored. Nancy's very genuine force of love penetrated the spirits of these little ones who didn't normally respond easily to people. They lit up at the sight of Nancy!

A big focus was to bring these children out into a freedom of expression. Pulling them into her arms, she would sing to them, affirm them, and speak to them one-on-one. It was as if there was no other person in the world at that moment, no other person of more significance than him or her. She was all about God to them, and they were all about God to her.

She taught them the Word, knowing that it was just as important for the very young to *know* God, as well as to know who they are in Christ. Intelligence level was not a hindrance. She taught them how to do warfare in the Spirit and that all authority is given to them by God. She made sure they could apply what they learned. As they enacted the Bible stories, they felt the reality of being soldiers in Christ. I watched them do spiritual warfare in their own way of expression. They were strong and bold. Nancy knew that God was just as real and powerful in those sweet children as in any noteworthy anointed Christian leader. These precious young believers were being mentored into being disciples of Christ. Her talents and creativity were remarkable and effective.

When Nancy learned of salvation and gave her life to Jesus, all she wanted was to be with Him! I have never before seen this longing in anyone. We had weekly "cell meetings" (Bible study ministry of our church at the time) in my home. Nancy played the piano and led the rest of us in worship. Time after time I would look at her and see that she just was not present with us, she wasn't. She quickly entered His Presence; and it was very apparent.

Nancy was the first of two sisters who died four and a half months apart. I wish the world could have known them. My prayer is that their mantles be left to the rest of us remaining siblings. Nancy was the most humble person I have ever seen. I observed her in many different circumstances. She was a solid witness. Linda was the most God-fearing person I have ever witnessed. I didn't understand what fearing God was until it was evident in her, deeply rooted. As she matured in Christ, she was firmly positioned on Galatians 2:20 for her challenges in life:

> *I have been crucified with Christ; and it is no longer I who live, but Christ lives in me; and the life which I now live in the flesh I live by faith in the Son of God, who loved me, and delivered Himself up for me.*

In her trials she was faithful, with a very serious and firm stand, to declare, "The fear of God is in me." Then she would quote this Scripture, maintaining that crucified life without allowing natural emotions and desires of self to take priority, not even for self-preservation. There is a later chapter on Linda.

My impressions of Nancy as humble and Linda as God-fearing started many years before their sicknesses and deaths. Death has a way of causing the negatives in your mind (of the deceased) to fade as their positives dominate the forefront. This was not that at all. These were my honest impressions of these ladies for a long time before they were even sick. Their strengths as Christians were striking and inspiring. It was all a result of their love for God, and their obedience to Him. Pure and true obedience is the Christian's part of the covenant for salvation. He gives us the grace *to live in obedience to Him.*

3

My Letter to the Family

Dear Father, (4/18/82, 4:34 a.m.)

I know it is a high price to pay if we want to see Your glory. But I know You can help me in all things and all sufferings can be joyful. Father, I want to see Your face. I am willing to pay that price. I want what You want for me. Help me to rejoice always. Teach me to live a life of praise. I love You and desire to see You,

Your humble servant,

Nancy

N ancy wrote this on the last page of the book of Job in her Bible. What follows is my letter to the family a couple of days after Nancy passed. I believed I saw the reason she died. It was not a failed faith, or anything of an existing hindrance, that blocked the healing. I touched up some of the grammar, re-worded it a little, and expounded (quite a bit in some places) on statements for clarification.

Dear Family:

What was the depth of Nancy's desire here? Did God put a desire in her heart and *allow* a journey that would take her straight to see His face and glory? Romans 8:18 was one of my favorite Scriptures that I prayed *faithfully* from the very beginning:

> *— the sufferings of this present day are not worthy to be compared to the glory yet to be revealed.*

It wasn't until her death that I understood just exactly what the glory would be. I believe Nancy's longing to see God's face is what this journey was all about. People *do* get sick on earth. Nancy got cancer. No doubt there was enough faith for her resurrection from death itself. But something so profound and glorious took place instead.

Genesis 5:24 *And Enoch walked with God; and he was not, for God took him* — I do parallel this with Nancy. Her walk was total dedication to Him, with an underlying desire to be home in Heaven. His extraordinary and supernatural power was more evident in her than in the rest of us.

> Hebrews 11:5–6 *By faith Enoch was taken up so that he should not see death; and he was not found because God took him up; for he obtained the witness that before his being taken up he was pleasing to God. (6) And without faith it is impossible to please Him, for*

*he who comes to God must believe that He is, and that
He is a rewarder of those who seek Him.*

(5) By faith Enoch ("dedicated") was taken up — It says "by faith." Did he believe for *that* to happen? We don't have all the detail. Were his life and faith so great that it pleased God and He took him up without his dying first? Why did not such a righteous man remain on earth to be a testimony of God, to be used for the Kingdom? Nancy was totally dedicated as well. She took every opportunity to lead people to the Lord, encouraged all in her path, and always had Bible studies that would develop fellow believers. She lived the commands of the Lord. Her life was a good definition of what it means to obey the call to Christians. Why was one of such great worth not left here to continue in an anointed ministry?

(5) so that he should not see death; and he was not found because God took him up — He just changed sides and passed over into Heaven. So did Nancy ("grace"); but unlike Enoch, she experienced a physical death. We expected a physical healing here on earth from her faith, and ours. Her cry to see His face and glory was etched in stone, deep in her heart. It was something she desired but never thought it would happen before she lived out a normal lifespan. As a Christian she wanted to please Him with all of her heart. When disease struck she honored Him with her faith in His healing promises. She NEVER complained, ever! (*I did a thorough word search through the book to make

sure that I didn't use superlatives in exaggeration. If it's used in the book, it *is* true to my observations.)

(5) for he obtained the witness that before his being taken up he was pleasing (Greek: "to gratify entirely") to God—She was faithful to utter honorable testimony to God's character and His promises. She gave only a good report and always said that He is a good God. To me, in spite of steady decline and then rapid end of life, this constant attitude was the epitome of faith. I believe God was completely gratified by what He saw in her. Just as He told Jesus, "Well done, My good and faithful servant," surely He told her as well.

(6) And without faith—Nancy never parted from her faith. Her full persuasion was that His Word is true. No matter how bad it got, she continued to believe and profess what the Bible said. She didn't tell us when she was in pain until the end stages. On one occasion she was sitting in the living room, and another family member heard what sounded like a pencil breaking. It was a tumor that outgrew its space in the bone and cracked it. If we didn't hear it, she probably would not have mentioned it.

(6) it is impossible ("without strength")—Her strength to go on was energized by her faith-in and love-for Him. She had periods of exceeding joy, and there were times that she battled the devil in warfare prayer with an uproar, despite her extremely weakened physical state. It was an incredible display of energy and power in those moments that took us by surprise.

(6) to please Him, for he who comes to God must believe that

He is—Nancy was already bold and faithful to pray the healing Scriptures for others in their sicknesses. Now battling for her own life, her endurance would be tested. The closer she got to Him, the more she knew His character, and the more she believed Him. Her whole Christian life was humbly and actively His. Colossians 3:1 is another Scripture that reminds me of her Christian focus:

> *If then you have been raised up with Christ, keep seeking the things above, where Christ is, seated at the right hand of God.*

Nancy reached this level of discipline. Years ago she made a remark to the effect that this world was an empty place and that she had no desire for it; but now it completely faded from her heart and lost all influence, even in attitude and emotion. People can be too sick to want anything, but she was in constant communion with the Lord and her longing to be with Him overshadowed all else.

As I was reading the Word to her one day, I paused to ask if she ever (in the past) had trouble with a certain battle in life from the verses we read. I don't remember what it was, but she looked at me and said, "Tena, I don't think about those things." It was with a very gentle, quiet, and humble spirit. She was so beautiful. The final result of the refining process, the testing as pure gold, was manifest. Several mature Christian attributes were displayed at that moment, and I was suddenly aware of her total separation from self, a true holiness. I was also ashamed and embarrassed at how shallow I was in ministry to her. (Added: I usually read the Psalms and passages on miracles. We had prayer intervals and Bible DVD's or praise music going around the clock.) Her need was the Psalms, and Scriptures on praise and God's love for her, more so than a daily Bible reading that included the dos and don'ts for life. Nothing of self existed at this point. Her mind was continually on God and the welfare of others. Her deepest concern was our sweet, precious little mama. 1 Peter 4:1–2 says it well:

> *Therefore, since Christ has suffered in the flesh, arm yourselves also with the same purpose, because he who has suffered in the flesh has ceased from sin, (2) so as to live the rest of the time in the flesh no longer for the lusts of men, but for the will of God.*

How true this was of Nancy. Toward the very end of her journey, her sole focus was the Lord. If we could just learn to live death to self as Christians to the point that all that matters is God! In Romans 6:6 we see the expectation of death to self:

> *—knowing this, that our old self was crucified with Him, that our body of sin might be done away with, that we should no longer be slaves to sin—*

(6) and that He is a rewarder of those who seek Him—I have consistently prayed, "God, You are a rewarder of those who diligently (KJV) seek You. Nancy diligently seeks You for her healing; and certainly the reward would be what she sought, her healing."

(Letter continues.)

Did her search for Him get so intense that she forsook her original desire for a healing and long more to be with Him? In the Greek, "diligently seek" means "to crave." Did she get to where she craved being in His presence?

> (Added: *I saw this at least by the day after she died. I remember telling of it at the wake. Someone recalled a statement by Joel Stockstill, one of my pastors. He said that sometimes when people are seeking God intensely during a sickness, somewhere along the path it results in a deeper closeness to Him; and they forsake the healing. There's a stronger desire to be with Him than to be healed. This may not be his exact words, but the meaning is there.)

John 12:23–25 *And Jesus answered them, saying, "The hour has come for the Son of Man to be glorified. (24) "Truly, truly, I say to you, unless a grain of wheat falls into the earth and dies, it remains by itself alone; but if it dies, it bears much fruit."*—I felt that the hour for Jesus to be gloried was upon her, that her *healing* was at hand. Nancy was already a very humble Christian; but the humility intensified with this long trial, revealing His unhindered, undeniable presence in her. She was still being used for His kingdom. I believed that a healing ministry was ahead and that a harvest was waiting. Perhaps she would have lived and had this ministry of healing the sick, but would have "remained alone" (as in this Scripture) *in view of maybe our not moving on to another level.* With her death the mantle is passed along to those who were close to her, to those who were diligent to fight the fight with her, as well as to those who were impacted by her ministry. The seeds she has scattered and watered will flourish. Rather than there being "one Nancy," maybe the Lord is raising up many more through us who would carry her mantle.

> (Added: this was written a few days after Nancy died. I was not saying that God took her, so that we'd assume (her) ministry. I was speculating on how He can use the circumstances to work all things together to the good. The above Scripture was very encouraging.)

(Letter continues.)

John 20:29 *Jesus said to him, "Because you have seen Me have you believed? Blessed are they who did not see, and yet believed."* – Our challenge: will we continue to believe in healing and miracles for others?

(Added: again, this was written the week she died. Little did I know that another sister would be on her deathbed about three weeks later with a diagnosis of leukemia.)

We did not see Nancy's healing, except for the perfect healing in Heaven. Will we still believe that healing is in His power for today? I really believe Nancy's desire to see His glory and His face (and being willing to pay the price) is ultimately what this journey was all about for her. In the face of steady decline, she maintained her faith with a focus on the stripes on Jesus' back. She continually confessed that His Word is true and that she believes Him. When she was admitted to the hospital in very painful times, she took the hand of her caretakers as they entered the room: "How are you? How's your family? Do you know Jesus?" On one of her many admissions to the hospital, her nurse said that the staff were amazed at how she presented. Usually patients at this stage were full of anger, cursing everyone who entered the room.

Our loving Father collected Nancy's life-long (as a Christian) tears of deep longing to be with Him. He took pleasure in her selfless life of service to Him. A manifested healing on this earth with a ministry to follow would have been an absolute, tremendous testimony that would have brought much glory to God; but it was "too small a thing" with which God would reward her. I imagine that He took her into the palms of His cupped hands, carried her straight up to His face, and said, "Come see My glory. See My Face. Healing on this earth is not enough of a reward for you." I believe His eyes were set on the burning desire of her heart, and that's how He chose to reward her:

> *Dear Father, (4/18/82, 4:34 a.m.)*
>
> *I know it is a high price to pay if we want to see Your glory. But I know You can help me in all things and all sufferings can be joyful. Father, I want to see Your face. I am willing to pay that price. I want what You want for me. Help me to rejoice always. Teach me to live a life of praise. I love You and desire to see You,*
>
> *Your humble servant,*
>
> *Nancy*

I wish the world would have known her; in a word, "humility." I believe she went way high up, **because He saw a sincere heart in 1982 and knew that she would indeed pay the price to go straight up to His face and glory.** Disease strikes the whole human race.

(Added: Nancy had a history of cancer and tumors. At fourteen years of age, she had a bone tumor surgically removed from her leg; and several years prior to 2005, she had another large growth on her leg that God miraculously healed, right before her eyes in the presence of others during a Bible study. They all saw it happen. It shrunk to nothing and never came back.)

Nancy journeyed through with great faith that would take her far beyond a healing here on earth. At the same time, He *does* work all things together for the good. I believe the sickness merged in with her journey to see His face and glory. Jesus' death was not in vain. Many are spared from hell. Neither need her death be in vain. When I pray for the family, I am still in the habit of coming to Nancy's name; and I pray that her death not be in vain, but that we here will take hold of her mantle and let it flourish for the Kingdom. I believe I have seen it already in at least one person. I would love to hear any difference you may see in your life. Anything that anyone would be willing to share of what the Lord has ministered to you, I would love to hear.

(Letter continues.)

Psalms 116:15 *Precious ("costly, highly-valued") in the sight of the Lord is the death of His Godly ones* — I believe that Nancy's faith in this journey was so precious to Him that He just had to have her up there with Him. He took her out of the world for His very own possession, to behold His face and glory. A servant like this is not so common. (I believe) she was very well-chosen to be rewarded with a high place in (His) glory. Just as Jesus went to the Cross without complaining, Nancy completed her journey without complaining. They both went into glory, having *completed their work on this earth.* Soon after she got saved, Nancy targeted the lost to spare them from hell. She was a magnet to the hurting, she had no idle days, Jesus was her life, and she did all unto His glory. Just as He carries out His work through each one of us, He can also designate any of us to carry out her mantle as well. I've never seen anyone as humble as Nancy. I really believe she was so one-with-God that the wonderful things He did through her didn't phase her. Rather, they were regular, extraordinary occurrences in her life. (She humbly and joyfully testified of His works, but she never boasted.) She was caught up in His world, denying her own.

I am not trying to elevate Nancy. I could only think that He Himself said, "My good and faithful servant." He is the author and finisher of our faith. His grace was sufficient for her to "pay the price."

(Added: again, this is not praising Nancy. Our lives must be about obeying God and allowing Him live to through us. An honest relationship with Him results in His character being produced in us. This brings Him glory and is not a thing of lifting up the person. Any expression of Nancy's humility is absolutely a reflection of *His* life revealed in her.)

Isaiah 57:1 *The righteous man perishes, and no man takes it to heart; and devout men are taken away, while no one understands*—I believe God didn't share the journey with us while it was happening, because we would have thought it needless to pray as we did. She believed His promises and proved herself to the end. We were in agreement with her and His Word, and that helped her to keep on going. We did not spoil her faith. It was righteousness to God and (I believe) what moved Him to answer that cry to see His glory. She was willing to believe Him, even though things got worse and worse, and more and more painful. What a faith in God! She paid the price. We held her hands up.

(End of letter to the family.)

Knowing that they all needed their own closure with God, I waited a few weeks before sharing the letter with the family. We believed with all of our hearts that she would live and were shocked when she died. I sought confirmation that what I had seen as the reason for her death was actually His truth, not my own way of thinking. After a couple of weeks, it was validated prophetically.

A co-worker, who knew I was standing for Nancy's healing, had the gift of prophecy. When I returned to work after a few days of funeral leave, I purposefully sat by her in the lounge during breakfast, hoping that she would have a word from the Lord to confirm the reason for Nancy's death. She immediately turned to me and said, "Tena, I had a dream about you last night, but I don't remember what it was." That was it. I didn't get the answer to my question; and she never asked how I was doing. There was no comment at all. Nothing of it came up. A few days later, I was sitting across the room from her and began to wonder why she never acknowledged Nancy's death. I walked up to her, stood by her side briefly, and thought, "Nahhh." I returned to my seat, but curiosity got the best of me. I walked up to her again and stood at her side for a couple of seconds, but turned away because of a lack of privacy. Without turning to me, this sister stopped me in my tracks and said, "Tenaaa, I think the Lord is talking to youuuu!" I said, "Nooo, I think it's me," and motioned for her to come to a more private place. As she approached me, she said, "Tena! This was the dream! You walked up to me twice and turned away twice! The Lord said, 'You know the answer. You already know the answer.'" She had the dream the *night before* I sat by her at breakfast, when I hoped to get a word from the Lord to confirm that what I thought was His reason for taking Nancy (instead of healing her) was His actual truth. My friend just could not remember the dream to be able to tell me then. God is so good.

When we get to Heaven and have all truth revealed, we *will* rejoice in His perfect reasons. We can trust Him. (The last chapter is this letter converted into a child's short story.)

4

Linda

We were again in the throes of believing and warfaring for another sister with a progno- sis of death. Our faith was not crushed or destroyed, not even diminished. It only became stronger; and we moved forward, expecting a miracle for Linda. Even in the most hopeless of circumstances, there's a God-given inclination toward hope. It's resilient and faithful to surface, along with a precious innate drive to do every-thing possible on behalf of our loved ones. Those are two things that we don't have to consciously rouse; but we do have to go beyond this by activating our faith and convert-ing that measure of hope into a strong and enduring faith.

In Judges 20:1–26 we see an example of Israel, even after being defeated twice, continuing to believe God for His intervention for victory. Background of the story is that the people of Gibeon wanted to fall under Israel's protection, so they deceived the tribe of Benjamin into thinking that they were Israel's allies. Without inquiring of God, Benjamin hastily received them into their clan. These Gibeonites later killed a Levite's concubine and disgraced the people. Israel wanted justice and to have this wickedness removed. But Benjamin refused to listen to them, their own brothers. Instead,

> *(14) "the sons of Benjamin gathered from the cities to Gibeah, to go out to battle against the sons of Israel."*

Benjamin had 26,700 men next to Israel's 400,000 men. That's pretty encouraging for Israel, but they weren't necessarily swayed by this advantage of having far greater numbers in manpower. They had intentions of going into battle, believing they would be victorious; but they weren't going to take action without inquiring of God first. No matter how powerful or favorable natural strengths or circumstances appear, they can still hurt or fail us. We must always seek God as our guide and answer, careful to be in His will.

> *(18) Now the sons of Israel arose, went up to Bethel, and inquired of God, and said, "Who shall go up first for us to battle against the sons of Benjamin?" Then the Lord said, "Judah shall go up first."*

It may sound minor, but their only question was who would go first. God's answer gave a favorable impression that their victory was certain. However, they were defeated.

Judges 20:22 *"—they encouraged themselves and arrayed for battle again in the place where they had arrayed themselves the first day."*—The loss didn't dislodge their hope, nor did it cause them to give up. There wasn't even an attitude that God failed them. They *encouraged themselves* in spite of the circumstances and dressed for battle, ready to be right back in the fight, keeping their eyes on God. When anything defies our faith, *we* must encourage ourselves in the Word, should we become disillusioned.

Judges 20:23 *And the sons of Israel went up and wept before the Lord until evening, and inquired of the Lord, saying, "Shall we again draw near for battle against the sons of my brother Benjamin?" And the Lord said, "Go up against him."*—Unfaltering in their solid faith in God, they came before Him weeping until evening. They were hopeful and ready to conquer Benjamin, their determination intensified, and they continued to seek His guidance before venturing out. He didn't say no to their inquiry the first time and now He as much as said to go. Once again, it seemed by the answer given that the victory was securely theirs; but they were defeated in this second attempt as well. They still trusted in God.

Judges 20:28 *"—Shall I yet again go out to battle against the sons of my brother Benjamin, or shall I cease?" And the Lord said, "Go up, for tomorrow I will deliver them into your hand."*—They really humbled themselves this time. Israel wept, fasted, and inquired of God. They were now being pulled in two different directions. On one hand they were wondering if they should quit. Was their faith wavering? I think not, because they were also asking if they should go out to battle again. I believe they were looking for His perfect will. They demonstrated a courageous and obedient heart on both counts. (1) Is Your perfect will that we completely deny self, give up, and not pursue victory through another battle? Is there another plan? (2) Do we continue in our pursuit and win? They were told twice to go and were defeated twice. Will it happen again? He told them clearly that Benjamin would be delivered into their hand; and they saw the effectiveness of their persistent faith.

Despite their being conquered twice, they weren't swayed. They kept their faith strong, regardless of the statistics. What if they withdrew after the first or second defeat? *They would have forfeited their impending victory.* They would never have known that their faith could accomplish such results. They would never have learned that faith must be enduring. They may not have gone to the next level.

We have to keep building on our faith, regardless of the outcome. When your faith does not result in your desired answer, cherish it. You may not see it, but your faith *is* going through a growth spurt. Every time we exercise our faith, it matters. It makes for the building blocks that are vital to our overall foundation and growth of faith that will impact future answers. In Hebrews 11:1 faith is defined as the assurance of things hoped for, the conviction of things not seen. A focus on circumstances will surely paralyze your faith. We must renew our minds to the *conviction of things not seen.* Our physical eyes are not able to see God and His Angels at work against the enemy in the spiritual realm. But there's a definite battle taking place on our behalf, especially when our faith is activated. I believe the greatest faith results from enduring the "no" answers, and continuing to trust God. Believing faith results only in "yes" answers can destroy your relationship with Him.

Back to Israel. Even though they saw nothing favorable or encouraging after their first two battles, they kept their hope in God. Our faith in Him must continue to grow, even when we don't see our desired results. The Word is full of His promises, and they *are* ours. We just don't know all that He knows. He alone is omnipotent and all-wise. I may not be privy to the end result; but I still adhere to His promises, unless otherwise directed. Ephesians 1:11 states that God works all things after the counsel of His own will (KJV). *He looks at the whole picture and acts accordingly.* When God doesn't answer our prayers as requested, He may be sparing us from worse circumstances of which we haven't any insights (examples in later chapter). We can trust that He knows best and be thankful for His intervention.

Just as with the Israelites, our faith carried on as well for our second battle (with terminal illness). Linda was practically on her deathbed before being diagnosed with leukemia. My immediate, distinct memory of Linda as we were growing up is that she was very selfless. She was the one who sacrificed her time to do certain non-routine chores around the house. The rest of us were happily about our own business, spared from duties that would intrude on our personal time of pleasure. One winter she was painting the living room for Mama. It was cold enough in this part of the house that she was wearing an overcoat. As I walked through, she paused to glance at me for a couple of seconds with a very humble countenance that reflected a steadfast death to self. In gentleness and quietness of spirit, she dipped her brush into the paint can and continued working without a word of complaint, not even questioning why I or any of the other seven siblings weren't helping. As an adult and with greater challenges, she remained that very selfless person; but now, as a Christian, she had a servant's heart that was devoted to pleasing Jesus by obedience to His example.

After college, Linda taught special-needs kids; and she absolutely loved it! Then she committed several years to homeschooling her own children. She always worked a part time job which took a lot of her weekends. When the boys were about six, eight, and ten, she resumed teaching first through eighth grades in the school system. Her time was consumed by the demands of a very busy lifestyle. I don't know that she made time for herself at all, more than likely not. Her youngest son, David, said that many of her sleep hours were given over to grading papers past midnight. Then she'd be up at 4:30 a.m. to read her Bible and pray for her family. Linda was a very strong prayer warrior over her household. She would never forfeit that opportunity of intercession.

Just as Nancy was focused on her little special-needs kids in Sunday school and readily reached out to others, Linda had that same drive and went beyond the normal duties of a school teacher. Dysfunctional homes are so common today, resulting in children having social issues through no fault of their own. Were their needs routinely met in their formative years? Were they affirmed? Did they have the necessary positive influences in their lives? Was their self-esteem built? Did they suffer abuse? Were they consistently taught right from wrong? Were they disciplined appropriately? Did their parents themselves model poor behavior? What was their socioeconomic status? Dysfunctions exist in all classes of people. I feel compassion for children who are repeatedly scolded for the faulty behavior that they've learned from the lifestyle of their own parents, day in and day out.

When meeting troubled children, it may be difficult for the adult to separate them from their behavior. Consequently, these children are generally *labeled and treated* as disruptive and rebellious trouble-makers. People stepping into their lives at this point often don't give them a chance. Rather, they *react* to their behavior in a negative way, inadvertently sustaining or increasing the child's dysfunctional ways. Linda was able to look past this and see the child as a victim caught up in a cycle: unfortunate

circumstances resulting in bad behavior that causes re-
buke by authorities all through life, which provokes the
behavior and more scolding. Sadly, the rebellion is rein-
forced when the root of the problem is not addressed in
a manner to heal the child. These little victims need to
be validated as a person and loved into good self-esteem.
Driven by compassion for them in their plight, Linda
recognized when children needed positive feedback and
consistently sought them out to show them that she cared
and valued them. In her eyes they were salvageable and
deserving of every bit of her effort to help promote a
healthy self-esteem. Realizing their behavior was a symp-
tom, she wanted to relieve them of their preconceived
idea that another adult would approach them with guards
up, ready with the reprimands. She knew just how to
reach them with the unconditional love of God. It was not
easy and there were challenges; but she was faithful and
successful.

One little fella who had the odds against him comes to
mind. He was problematic, rendering him vulnerable to
an unfortunate path in life. But Linda spent quality time
with him, faithfully ministering love and understanding.
She validated him with positive affirmations of who he
really was inside. The character of this little man started
to change, and a sweet spirit began to emerge. He was
being transformed. Proverbs 23:7 says that as we think
within, so we are. The fruit of her labors remained for
years. Not knowing anything about him, I was impressed

and touched by his compassion, sweetness, politeness, and respectfulness during his conversation with Linda's youngest son at her funeral. A co-worker of Linda's later pointed out that he was one of the children changed by her personal commitment to love him unconditionally and help develop his self-esteem.

The week before Nancy's death, Linda came to spend the weekend with her and to help with the around-the-clock care. She intended to stay up all night in prayer for Nancy after a two-and-a-half-hour drive from her home. The next day she said it was difficult and that she didn't make the whole night. I remember looking at her and thinking that she looked tired and humble. I attributed it to her being a busy mother of seven children (one was away at college and another was married), being a full-time teacher, having a part-time job and other commitments that filled her weekends, having a long drive, and *staying up a good portion of the night*. Nancy died the following Monday. When Linda returned for the funeral, I was struck again by her being quiet and looking tired, but attributed it to the circumstances. We were all drained.

Several days after Nancy's burial, Linda thought that she came down with the flu. It wasn't until her daughter, Jamie, later developed the same symptoms that they went to the doctor together. Even though they were both treated for the flu, Jamie recovered, but Linda continued to get progressively worse. Her concern now turned to Mama, since she stayed with her for a few days after the funeral.

Mama's very health-conscious and meticulous about taking her medicines. She's been faithful to get the pneumonia and flu vaccinations to avoid sickness in her old age; but Linda feared she must have actually been contagious during her stay with Mama, putting her at risk.

Even though Linda was not feeling well at all, she ignored her personal needs and pushed herself in an attempt to fulfill school obligations: tests, report cards, etc. Pushing past her limit, she was found asleep on her desk in the classroom, prompting a follow-up visit to the doctor. It was Thursday, November 10. On her initial visit, the doctor gave her a good dose of medicine to knock out the flu, but to no avail. Concerned that something very serious was threatening her health, the doctor gave her orders to go to the lab immediately, hoping to secure the results before the weekend. Just the trip to the doctor's office depleted all of her energy and overrode her every intention of going to the lab. She went straight home, put the doctor's orders on the counter, and went to bed. It was all that she could do. Since Linda was not a complainer, we were clueless of just how poorly she felt until later. Our only thought was that she was tired and needed rest. Sylvia suggested that maybe she was suffering from exhaustion and encouraged her to take a couple of months off from teaching to recuperate.

Mama became worried about Linda's prolonged illness with the flu, and couldn't help thinking about past epidemics of various strains of the virus. Knowing that something was terribly wrong, she called different family members to check on Linda. Kitty then drove Mama the two-and-a-half-hour distance, so that she could lay her own eyes on her. Too sick to move, Linda was confined to bed over the weekend, suffering gout-like pain in one of her ankle joints. That's symptomatic of leukemia when the bone marrow is overcrowded by very fast-producing abnormal white blood cells that are competing for space and nutrients belonging to normal, healthy cells. Things of the disease are now advancing rapidly in her body.

On Monday, November 14, the doctor expected some lab results, thinking she had blood drawn following her office visit. Not receiving any, he called her to stress the need to be evaluated now. But with a sick child at home and her maternal drive in high gear, she was hesitant to leave the house. At that point, Linda had to be made to understand that her condition was severe. The next day her WBC resulted a critical value of 596,000 (the normal range is 4,500-10,000). Linda was diagnosed with acute AML leukemia, which has the same symptoms as the flu. She was admitted to the hospital, dying. It literally took her deathbed to coerce Linda to consider herself. But her thoughts and broken heart remained on her kids.

Her precious children (David, Timmy, James, Sarah, Jamie, Tina, and Nancy) were young, ranging in age from eleven to twenty-four, to be losing a parent. Her husband, Mike, would soon find himself a single parent.

We went right into believing for her healing just as we

did Nancy's. Linda was in the hospital from the day she was admitted until her death. Several family members took turns staying with her for a few days at a time. We had to be very cautious of what we brought into the room, practice good hand-washing, and stay clear of any hint of illness. At first I was a little apprehensive of possibly being contagious at any moment, when the symptoms of sickness didn't yet surface for a warning to stay away. That was the first year that I gave in to the annual free flu vaccination at work, but I was still on guard. Because children are easy catchers and transmitters of disease, especially at that time of the year, her kids were hardly allowed into the room.

When Mama and I made our four-and-a-half-hour trips to spend a few days with Linda, we stopped halfway to see her children. During our visit, we made videos of them for her. On return-trip home, we brought a short footage of Mom back to them. Very vivid in my mind is the beautiful image of her delight as she watched our little Christmas celebration with her kids. After a few minutes of the video, I turned to glance at her. In an instant, I was deeply and warmly impacted with the sweetest and most endearing display of a mom's love-for and pride-in her children. Dressed in her light blue robe, with a white terry turban on her bald head, sitting upright in the middle of her hospital bed, arms wrapped around her knees pulled to her chest, she was totally mesmerized by her children, gleefully relishing every detail of the video, beaming throughout the entirety of the movie. I was spellbound as I observed her eyes quickly scan the screen to examine every detail, determined not to miss a thing. Forever in my remembrance is the broad, fixed, gaping smile on her face—a beautiful display of the overflow of her heart. (I love to recall that image. It still impacts me the same way.) In complete oblivion to anyone else in the room, she appeared to be in her very own theater, gratified and energized by this very endearing movie that allowed her the only opportunity to enjoy her kids in their unavoidable absence at Christmas. I am just saddened that I was not able to capture all of this for her children, since the camcorder was in use for her viewing.

After five and a half months of hospitalization, Linda died. One of the Oncologists said that leukemia had been raging in her body for at least a month before the diagnosis was made. They didn't expect her to live through the first night of her admission, much less all those months. The doctors were amazed to find her alive from day to day, sitting up, greeting them cheerfully (that was Linda). The staff appropriately nicknamed her "Sparkle." She was a blessing to them and they loved her. "Sparkle" left this earth with a very visible remaining twinkle at the corner of her eyes. Her countenance was so sweet.

One would think that we would have been "taken down," and our faith destroyed. BUT! God took us to a place that I never knew existed, a place of powerful grace and very sweet peace. We were still in a strong place.

His comforting presence and love were right there for us. Apparently there's no limit to the amount of peace available. It correlates to the degree of suffering. I am not saying that I wasn't devastated and that it was not painful. There was no escape from the hurt and grief. But my *faith* was not touched or lessened, and I had a keen awareness of His love. For a relatively short period of time, I didn't have the same level of vigor within to pray for the needs of others, but it was restored. At first it felt awkward. That was the only set-back that I experienced. I lost two very precious sisters whom I loved very much, but God showed Himself strong on my behalf. (We also lost a precious brother-in-law almost three weeks prior to Nancy's death. There's a later chapter on Walter.)

5

Mama

**Mama holding boutonnieres given to her
by Linda's sons after their graduations—
Image courtesy of Joylynn Breaux.**

Mama's hands are so beautiful, always busy for her loved ones, and highly motivated to meet any need encountered. They've always been a reflection of her heart as wife and mother (grandmother and great-grandmother as well), uncovered a wide variety of gifts and talents, and released her soothing influence in times of illness and pain. I am reminded of this Scripture:

> *The Lord will command the blessing in your barns and*
> *in all that you put your hand to*—Deuteronomy 28:8

Her soft and gentle touch imparted a strong sense of well-being, comfort, and security to the one not feeling so well. Curled up in bed and too sick to move during certain illnesses, I slept for hours and was awakened only by her cool, soft hand as she placed it ever so lightly on my forehead to check for a fever. The love that I knew at that moment prevailed over the effects of my illness and overshadowed how poorly I felt.

> *And let the favor of the Lord our God be upon us; and*
> *do confirm for us the work of our hands; yes, confirm*
> *the work of our hands*—Psalm 90:17

I really believe this verse is a promise automatically fulfilled for mothers. Their level of commitment, passion to protect, and boundless love for their children are unsurpassed. God forms and weaves the inward parts of women with these unique qualities. After giving birth, her heart is overcome by the reality of her infant's delicacy, innocence, helplessness, and vulnerability. This imprint never fades. Her unmistakable and beautiful God-given natural instinct to nurture and protect manifests; it's set into action. She's well-equipped with an abundant supply of very deep emotions correlating to her children's roller-coaster events throughout a lifetime, everything from joy to sadness. Continual sacrifices are a given, but she doesn't consider anything a sacrifice. Even in the most threatening of circumstances, the protective instinct kicks in at full capacity and is all-consuming. All fear of personal harm is instantly overcome if it's a matter of saving her child. Then, when a mother carries sorrow for her offspring of *any* age, there's a great stirring at the core of her being. It all comes back: the delicacy, the innocence, the helplessness, and the vulnerability of her "baby." A tenacious drive to save that baby overtakes her, no matter the cost.

Mama delivered nine children in nine years. Her tenth was a stillborn, which is still a sad memory for her. Three months of the year she was not pregnant, and most of the other nine months were filled with nausea and vomiting. Through this she had an infant, a one-year-old, and a two-year-old, all in cloth diapers that she washed by hand and scrub board until she got a ringer washer. That's just one of the numerous duties interrupted by chasing after us for our protection as we explored and endangered ourselves. There weren't an abundance of educational toys in those days; and we didn't have a television to captivate our attention, keeping us still in one spot for a while. Mama was alone with us children most of the time.

In their early marriage, Daddy worked away from home for weeks and months at a time, rendering Mama the life of a single mom. They married in her country, Caracas, and soon moved to the states, leaving behind access to her family's help in times of need. It would be almost thirty years before she would see them again. Daddy's siblings also had large families and were busy in their own households. Mama didn't drive and was not yet fluent in English, but she managed to establish several good friendships with the neighbors, who were faithful to come through for her.

The family kept growing. There was always an infant, a one-year-old, and a two-year-old until there were also the ages of three, four, five, six, seven, and eight. What a tremendous undertaking to care for the high level of activity in these ages: the mischievousness, picking, fighting, accidents and near accidents, fast pace, school, different personalities and needs, crankiness, hunger, loudness, sickness, etc. Mama was alone most of the time. How did she manage and remain emotionally sound? She's always been a woman of courage and amazing strength, forever denying herself. Very little rest was the norm for her, and there were many times when she was deprived of sleep altogether.

For the last thirty-nine years, the family always had two babies in diapers at the same time. Having nine children and twenty-two grandchildren kept Mama pretty busy, trying to balance her very limited time between *pleasure with* and *needs of* the different families. What a balancing act! Impossible to be everywhere, it became necessary to prioritize by needs first. Bless her heart, she used to caution us saying, "There's not one of my children of whom I could ever say I wish was not born. Y'all are here and I love each one very much; but please don't have too many children." It was not with a tone of complaint, just quiet wisdom from experience. It would be much later that I realized she was referring to the larger the family, the more complex the household, and the more the demands. It was inevitable, and there was still just "one you" to manage it all. Certainly for the grandmother, the greater the odds were that she would be needed simultaneously in two or more different directions. She had a strong instinct when there was a serious situation needing her direct attention, and was faithful to forsake all else to be there. We had very little awareness of all that Mama carried. In today's world there are an abundance of conveniences that weren't available to her. Yet, it's common to hear parents say that two children are hard enough to handle in this day and age. I am forever grateful that she kept a firm, solid hand on us in her efforts to raise us right. She did an excellent job.

Of all the relationships involving the loss of a loved one, I think the hardest and saddest is the loss of a child, especially when the parent is aged. Mama spent years toiling over Nancy and suffered her loss. Then she spent months toiling over Linda and suffered her loss as well.

She was also carrying a burden for her first daughter, Ana, who was widowed just three weeks before Nancy died. It was a very strenuous five-year period for Mama. Brokenhearted with the three back to back losses, and not having the time to even start the grieving process, she was prey to a very sensitive, vulnerable, and fragile position. She was in need of our love, understanding and compassion, our ears, arms, and tears, honor and respect. Her heart was ripped out twice in a very, very short period. She was well-deserving of a sanctuary of peace and rest, and the time to heal. None of us came close to any degree of her sorrow. Ours paled in comparison. Just the thought of losing a child is terrifying; but Mama experienced that reality of extreme hardship. She has always been a very strong woman of courage, enduring many trials with an admirable strength. God's grace is limitless.

In 2005 and 2006, Mama lost two daughters to cancer five and a half months apart. Nancy was the first to get sick. Mama read several books, researching all possibilities to help fight this disease. She chose foods with plenty of antioxidants, cooked with herbs and spices, was constantly cleaning and dusting, got rid of chemicals in the house and didn't allow any outside, washed the clothes with hydrogen peroxide, rinsed her dishes in vinegar, juiced fresh fruits and vegetables, etc. She labored all day long, literally. Many times after Mama spent hours cooking and cleaning, Nancy was just not able to eat what was so carefully prepared. This was pretty much the norm, but Mama never gave up. She would go right back into the kitchen to prepare something else of equal value. There was *never* a complaint. She rose above discouragement and continued to persist in her endeavors; and even though her heart was breaking, she derived her energies from the hope that her child would live. A mother's love is very strong and durable.

A little less than a month after Nancy's death, Mama was faced with another daughter in a dying state. Linda was hospitalized in a distant city and was going to remain there. It's a hard thing to be separated from your sick child, especially when they're terminally ill. For example, on one of Nancy's admissions to the hospital, her arm felt like it was on fire. She desperately wanted to die. While containing her need to scream from the extreme pain, she looked at me frantically and said, "Tena, get Mama out of here! Please!" Nancy was just being admitted to her room, and we had to step out into the hallway for a minute anyway. I offered Mama to take her home for a little while to get some rest, so that she could come back later, refreshed and ready for a possible long night. Another family member would be there until we returned. Understandably, she did not want to leave for one minute. Honesty was best at that point. Things were critical and no one needed to beat around the bush. They were very concerned about each other. "Mama, Nancy would rather you not see her in pain. She wants you to go home for now. She's not able to freely express herself (the pain) with you here, because she's trying to spare you." In her strong Spanish accent, she was very resolute, "I no leabie." There was no question of the right thing to do. It would be criminal to deny Mama her rightful place at that moment. She knew what she would be facing. As bad as that was, it would be worse to be away from her baby. I believe we become helpless little infants in the hearts of our moms when our sickness may lead to severe complications or death. Their only focus is to be at your side, doing everything possible to comfort or rescue you. These are the times that we are "babies" to our mamas.

I first realized this several years ago when in a season of ministry to an elderly Christian lady in her late eighties. She was losing her eyesight and was very disappointed that she was no longer able to read the Scriptures for herself. She had a tape recorder, so I brought her my Bible on tapes. We put different large colored dots on the but-tons—green on the play button, yellow on rewind, blue on eject, and red on stop. We hoped that she would see the large bold colors well enough to function independently. Unfortunately, it didn't work out as we expected. The only other option was my calling her every morning at her desired time of 5:00 a.m. (Those thirteen months were wonderful! There's just something to reading the Bible out loud.) I also wrote my phone number in huge print on paper and taped it across her wall, should she need me. Her sixty-two-year-old son spent the day in New Orleans for Mardi Gras and was not back by 4:30 p.m. This caused her to worry, which prompted a frantic call to me. "Sister Lydia, he's a grown man!" "Ah know it, but he's still mah behbeh!"

Back to Mama. During Linda's illness there was no choice in the matter of separation. We made many four-and-a-half-hour trips to be with her in the hospital for three or four days at a time. Sometimes Mama stayed through when the sisters and sisters-in-law switched out. She returned home at intervals when Mike would be there. Her labors were non-stop: she pureed organic fruits and vegetables, sterilized jars and canned the food, bought and washed clothes for her, etc. She got back to Linda as quickly as she could.

Mama never complained about the timing of all the sickness and deaths. She just kept on going, very driven to do all that she possibly could to help heal her child. Her constant labors were endless for Linda until she died after a few months of being diagnosed with leukemia.

With Linda's death there was an added dimension to Mama's pain, a deep sorrow for the children in their loss. It was another hurt all in itself. (Thank God, children are more resilient than our hurting hearts realize.) I believe the maternal instinct for mothers doesn't stop with her own children, but penetrates right down through the next generation, connecting to her grandkids as well. It's strong, very focused, and full of wisdom and undistracted love.

What we siblings suffered was not comparable at all to Mama's anguish. *She lost a daughter who left young children behind.* The instinct is to carry on for Linda, being available in whatever capacity. That's the heartbeat of a mother and grandmother. It just is.

Mama almost lost her own life (hemorrhaging after a stillbirth) when she had nine children under the age of eleven. This close call was a terrifying experience: she saw her babies motherless and was very apprehensive at just the thought of this ever happening. When you barely escape a tragedy like that, you actually experience a degree of the emotions as if it did happen.

Linda spoke with Mama about her concern for her children, should she die. With a tremendous amount of compassion and a broken heart, Mama *knew* what she felt. In their conversations, Linda got a sense of security that Mama would have a part in their lives and be of good influence. She's faithful to be involved with the children and grandchildren as much as possible when the occasions present. Mothers never completely get over the deaths of their children. Forever in Mama's heart will be the driving force to be there for Linda's kids, not only because she loves them very much, but because of the natural loving maternal instinct to do for Linda (and the children) in her absence. It was a promise made that gave Linda peace.

After the deaths, Mama recalled a dream she had long ago, in which she was holding a bouquet of long-stemmed red roses. Two of them were broken and hanging down. She realized they were Nancy and Linda. From the time they died, Mama kept a red rose in the foyer for each of the girls. Once wilted and dried out, they were replaced with freshly picked roses. This went on for years. I believe she quit when her heart had some amount of healing. She now forever has the rosebud boutonnieres that Linda's three sons gave her (Mama) from their high school graduations.

Well, life has gone on for Mama. The Lord blessed her with many talents that she never allowed to lay dormant. Her beautiful hands unveiled her creativity on numerous projects throughout the years. I still love to watch them at work, making the things of her imagination a reality. When we children were teenagers, she managed every phase of several weddings: making the bride's wedding dress as well as those of the bridesmaids, tackling the intricate complexities of the bride's head piece and veil, decorating the church and reception hall, catering the food, and making the wedding and groom's cakes. The bouquets, boutonnieres, and corsages were skillfully designed and made by Mama. Without the convenience of dried flowers back then, she made them herself from crepe paper dipped in melted wax, forming each petal, leaf, and stem. Decades later at eighty-six years old, she made all of the floral arrangements for my niece's wedding in June 2011. One of Jamie's bridesmaids married before she did and offered all of her arrangements that yielded a huge assortment of beautiful dried flowers.

As I checked in on Mama one afternoon, I was saddened by what I saw. Behind her house is a very large shed that served as her workshop. She was sitting adjacent to the opened door, utilizing the sunlight to enhance her vision. Original floral arrangements from the previous wedding were intact and strewn about the floor, stacked on top of each other, leaving very little walking space. It was an overwhelming sight to me; but she was calm as she worked for hours, extracting a flower here and a flower there from the very secure tight arrangements. It was an obvious work of love in action.

When Mama took her dinner break, I stayed behind with a determination to take every arrangement apart and separate each flower into its own type. After six straight hours, the clutter transformed into a floral shop that lacked for nothing! For months Mama worked from morning till night, taking short breaks as needed. She frequently worked longer periods of time than she should have. On my way home from work, I would drop by to see how things were progressing and find a beautiful array of several incredibly gorgeous creations. She once told me over the phone that she changed the arrangements around. "Oh no, Mama, those were absolutely gorgeous and perfect!" At that moment I was very disappointed that something of such beauty was destroyed and felt that she was spinning her wheels, only to find that the replacement surpassed the beauty of the original design. I was now filled with excitement in anticipation of her innovations from day to day! It was mind-boggling that a woman of this age could sit there and skillfully whip out these beautiful creations with such ease. From time to time I tell her she could've been a multi-millionaire, had she pursued a career. There's not a doubt in my mind!

Mama took only a couple of hours to assess the church where Jamie was to marry. She also looked at the reception hall that was quite a distance from the church. After that one time, her plan was in place. She never went back to reassess the church or reception hall.

There were three sections of pews, rather than two, which meant decorating two aisles and having to do a little problem-solving for the bride's walk. Mama even noticed many pedestals several feet high on the side walls, about fifteen feet apart, on which she placed lit candles in clear decorative vases adorned with cascading flowers. It was all gorgeous and completed to perfection. Nothing was forgotten: the pews, altar, front foyer, reception hall, etc. How she coordinated everything is bewildering. The church worker who provided access to the church was amazed and said that she never saw the church decorated so beautifully.

This huge (for anyone) achievement was a turning point in restoring Mama to the joys of life. The elderly need to do as much as they can independently for as long as possible. But at eighty-eight, I get concerned about her doing too much for a consecutive number of days with relatively little rest. When I tell her of my concern, she expresses enjoyment in her work, grateful that she's able. She may get tired, but she thrives on it and knows that she'll get the needed rest at adequate intervals.

Mama has always been thankful for each one's well-being and good fortune throughout the years. She's consistently prayed every night for *each family member* just before going to sleep. It remains a faithful habit to this day for our large clan. She now has twenty-six great-grandchildren, and that number will continue to grow. There are even others she regards as her own. I am very thankful for a mother, grandmother, and great-grandmother, all in one, who honestly has a very deep and genuine caring heart for each one of us. She amazes me. I will always be appreciative of the mother God gave me.

Her children rise up and bless her — Proverbs 31:28

6

Walter

Although my brother-in-law, Walter, always criti-
cized Christianity, he became a Christian at the
very end of his life. Ana received salvation a
few years into their marriage and shared her new faith
with him. He was resistant from the beginning, saying
things like: "Christianity is a crutch that I don't need,"
and "Christianity is for weak people." He even professed
to be an atheist. In spite of his negativity against the Word,
Ana upheld a verbal and visible witness before him. He
became angry, aggressive, rebellious, and antisocial; and
tried to prevent her from attending church, partly because
he felt that he lost some of her attention.

He once took a cross off the wall and threw it down,
which hurt Ana deeply; but regardless of his ongoing
rebellion, she firmly attested to God's love for him. He
didn't believe there was a Heaven. Ana affirmed that there
is and said that she believed he himself would be there.
Faithful to his firm mindset at the time, he assured her

that he would *not* be. She didn't express discouragement and never gave up.

I can remember telling her way back then, "If we have to pray for his salvation for thirty years, we'll pray for thirty years." Ana has a faithful friend, Patty, who joined in with her in this effort, enduring those years as well. What a treasure! It's a God-given responsibility to carry the burden for lost souls and intercede for those other than just our loved ones. The opportunities surround us. Faith and prayer paid off for Walter in the last two weeks of his life. This is a good example of not seeing God answer in our time and that it doesn't mean He won't answer at all. We have to continue believing, persevering with a steadfast endurance for something as critical as a loved one's salvation.

Walter was stricken with cancer a year before Nancy died. Aware of her grueling years of treatments, the ups and downs, and just how horrible a journey it was, he immediately vowed that he would beat his cancer. His prognosis was six months, but he lived an additional seven, the most critical phase of his entire life. It was near the end of this time that his heart softened toward God.

There was a lot of healing and restoration between him and Ana in the thirteen months. Contrary to his silent treatment during their marriage, she now sensed his genuine love and appreciation as she cared for him. There were apologies, humility, sweetness, and kindness. Early in his sickness when he had high hopes of recovery,

Walter told Ana that he wanted to take her on a cruise to Hawaii. Sadly, his life continued to slip away.

They spent one evening in conversation while they overlooked the horizon of the city through a large window in his hospital room. The lights were out; and it was quiet and peaceful. The beautiful glistening city lights in the absence of sounds from the city enhanced their already tranquil environment and fostered a greater awareness of the bond of peace and appreciation between them. He talked in detail of vacations that he wished they had enjoyed together. Walter closed out their evening stating that he felt as if they actually experienced the vacation. As Ana told the story, I sensed a soft, sweet, "romantic" quality.

When two people sincerely ask forgiveness from each other and are truly forgiven for past wrongs, the relationship is miraculously restored. The years of discord between Ana and Walter became a vapor; and they now shared a mutual caring and gentleness toward each other. They became closer than they've ever been.

Nancy (hurting, limping, and using a cane) visited Walter about half way through his sickness and witnessed to him about salvation. He was attentive and allowed her to pray for him. Towards his last couple of months, he started asking questions about God. At one point he asked Ana what the sunshine in her religion was and asked for her to pray for him as well. He held the hand of one of my brothers (Arkie) for forty-five minutes and asked for prayer. While another brother and his wife (Tommy and

Te) visited him, they also had the privilege of praying for him. His spirit was very sweet.

When Walter was discharged to home on hospice care, he saw an Angel as he was being put to bed. We believe that he gave his life to Jesus just a short two weeks before he died. His language became more so that of a believer, and a beautiful, visible peace covered him. He was a transformed man.

I always prayed, "God get him saved, then heal him." What if God healed him of cancer right after salvation? What if he recalled vowing to heal himself, and believed that he did? Would he have decided that he did not need God, and then walked away from his salvation before any real depth or dedication took place? How tragic that would have been for his eternity. In Matthew 13:20–21, Jesus explained the parable of one of the four seeds:

> *"And the one on whom seed was sown on the rocky places, this is the man who hears the word, and immediately receives it with joy; (21) yet he has no firm root in himself, but is only temporary, and when affliction or persecution arises because of the word, immediately he falls away."*

This man's salvation did not last. He had no firm root and fell away. I am so grateful that the Lord took Walter before this could've happened to him. God rescued His precious son from this world before the enemy had any opportunity to reclaim his soul.

7

In His Omniscience and Sovereignty

I am a firm believer that any Christian, who desires to be healed, should stand solid for their healing. Even though there are many instant miracles happening as people lay hands on the sick, chances are that God will not heal you without your faith in action. He may perform the miracle in a moment, or it may take a long period of time with a steadfast faith. When it doesn't manifest, God has a reason that's very close to His heart. Refrain from the temptation to automatically blame it on sin or a lack of faith. Don't do that to yourself or to anyone else. It's clear that Hezekiah's death would have prevented terrible things.

During his illness, it was prophesied that he was going to die; but he wanted to live and wept bitterly before God. So fifteen years were added to his life (2 Kings 20:1–6, 21). In addition to this, God informed Hezekiah that He would deliver him and the city from the king of Assyria and that

He would also defend the city. That was something good that happened with the extension of his life. However, during this same time, he also fathered a son who was extremely evil. Manasseh (his son) shed the innocent blood of multitudes of people and caused Judah to sin:

> *In those days Hezekiah became mortally ill. And Isaiah the prophet the son of Amoz came to him and said to him, "Thus says the Lord, 'Set your house in order, for you shall die and not live.'" (2) Then he turned his face to the wall, and prayed to the Lord, saying, (3) "Remember now, O Lord, I beseech Thee, how I have walked before Thee in truth and with a whole heart, and have done what is good in Thy sight." And Hezekiah wept bitterly. (4) And it came about before Isaiah had gone out of the middle court, that the word of the Lord came to him, saying, (5) "Return and say to Hezekiah the leader of My people, 'Thus says the Lord, the God of your father David, I have heard your prayer, I have seen your tears; behold, I will heal you. On the third day you shall go up to the house of the Lord. (6) And I will add fifteen years to your life, and I will deliver you and this city from the hand of the king of Assyria; and I will defend this city for My own sake and for My servant David's sake.'"*

> *(21) So Hezekiah slept with his fathers, and Manasseh his son became king in his place*—his son would not have been

born if Hezekiah wasn't given the added fifteen years of life.

2 Kings 21:1–2 *Manasseh was twelve years old when he became king, and he reigned fifty-five years in Jerusalem; and his mother's name was Hephzibah. (2) And he did evil in the sight of the Lord*—Hezekiah desperately wanted to live longer, but had he known what would unfold, he may have foregone his request.

(16) Moreover, Manasseh shed very much innocent blood until he had filled Jerusalem from one end to another; besides his sin with which he made Judah sin, in doing evil in the sight of the Lord—How grievous! The masses of people who died! The masses who were led into sin! Even though Hezekiah walked before God in truth with a whole heart and did what was good in His sight, his added fifteen years resulted in a very unfortunate, tragic future for multitudes of people, because of Manasseh's evil. There's more to consider than just the one person standing for a healing. If God chose to deny Hezekiah's request, for the purpose of circumventing this whole catastrophic era, no one would have known that his death was *not* because of a failed faith, nor would they have known that they were being spared from the evil of a son *who would've been born to him in that time.*

How does this all apply to us? It's possible for anyone with faith to be healed of disease, because of the stripes Jesus suffered on His back. We have promises for every need, but many times we don't see the desired results of our faith and prayers. We are not omniscient and may not understand why our petitions, such as for a healing, are not answered as hoped. In His omniscience, He sees the whole picture in our lives. In His sovereignty, He has full right to the final answer to do what's best. It goes far beyond just us and our hopes for our loved ones. He knows exactly how things will play out in the future.

I'm sure there are *many various* reasons why we don't see healings take place in the midst of beautiful, strong faith in action. (1) Would a multitude of people *indirectly* be adversely affected, for some reason, throughout generations to come? It happened with the extension of Hezekiah's life. (2) What about the path in life the healed one will take once they recover? Will they turn from Him at a later date? (3) Is God sparing them from something else in life? In His great mercy, He may be rescuing a believer from some decision and consequence, such as the one-year-old baby who grew up and committed murder. In John 5:14, Jesus later told the paralytic, who was miraculously healed, *"Behold, you have become well; do not sin anymore, so that nothing worse may befall you."* (4) It's hard to comprehend God's taking a Christian home in the midst of their unwavering faith and righteousness before Him. Did their level of faith and intimacy with God just carry them over to the other side (Heaven)? If I reached the place of wanting to be with Him, I would not want anyone's faith to detain me here on earth. (5) I would imagine there are many reasons that supersede our finite minds; and we will not have the revelation until we get to Heaven.

I believe the Lord allowed me to see the explanations for five untimely deaths. They are all different and specific to each person. I related only three of them (a one-year-old baby, Nancy, and Walter). The others are not mine to tell. Some of the glimpses we get are to remain in our hearts, respecting its beauty and holiness, while acknowledging the tremendous love of God.

An Infant

In God's omniscience, He saw that a one-year-old baby boy would commit murder as an adult. This baby died on the operating table while undergoing surgery. The chief surgeon told the mother that they did all they could, but were not able to save him. In wrath, she shook her fist up at God saying, "He's mine, he's mine! You can't take him!" The assistant surgeon then came out with the report that the baby is alive. He grew up, committed murder, and went to the electric chair. Did he take Jesus as his personal Lord and Savior before death? I hope so. Or did he go to hell? As a baby, Heaven would have been his. God had a sovereign right to take that one-year-old baby, in order to spare him from the eternal consequences of any unrepentant sinful decisions in life. Then there's the victim and his family to consider. Was he ready to face the Judgment? Consider his family and friends, the extreme sadness and grief from something that should not have happened. How did it disrupt their lives? What about the breakdown of their support system and the absence of his role in the home as husband, father, protector, and provider? How many people depended on this person and in what ways? There are multifaceted implications of this one devastating act that could've been prevented. We have to be so careful to respect His sovereignty when our hopes are shattered, or we can get on dangerous territory.

What if this was the scenario: a dedicated Christian mother would have pleaded for his life while honoring God as God. Yet, the baby died in spite of this mother's pure and solid faith. She's confused, shocked, and feels abandoned by God. She questions His Word and begins to experience bitterness, maybe even extreme anger at God for a time. Eventually she would be restored to a very loving and reverent relationship with the Lord. She gives God His place. At some point she is healed and her relationship with Him is deeper and richer than she ever thought possible. In her anger she never walked away from God. She still loved Him.

Given the choice, I think that any mother with an understanding of eternal consequences would willingly choose her child's death over his forever existence in the horrible pits of hell. Once in Heaven and knowing the truth, she can truly say, "Thank You, Father, for sparing my precious, innocent baby from chancing life on earth and somehow getting to the place of murdering someone.

Thank You for not restoring his life in order to free me of my anguish. You spared him from *eternal* hell. You rescued him from what would have been if he were to live." In the midst of pain and grief, things may be incomprehensible and senseless. Do trust that He may know of an impending tragedy that bears much greater suffering than the loss of a baby.

> *The righteous man perishes, and no man takes it to heart; and devout men are taken away, while no one understands. For the righteous man is taken away from evil*—Isaiah 57:1

Nancy

In God's omniscience, He knew that cancer would be one of Nancy's trials in life. satan utilized brutal attacks against her body in an effort to destroy her incorruptible faith. But it proved to be untouchable and immovable. She never strayed from a path of total surrender to Him. He also knew that more than anything—and at any cost—she wanted to see His glory, and that she *would* pay the price. With apparent determination, she fought the devil, even in her weakened state, declaring that by His stripes she's healed. All through her journey, she confessed that God is a good God. She never got angry and never gave up. In His sovereignty, He had the right to take Nancy, no matter how great the faith was that rose up before Him, because He saw the sincerity of her life-long heart's desire to be with Him. He gave the much greater reward toward that very end in itself.

One of our siblings heard her say, softly and sweetly, "When? . . . Monday? . . . Okay." That Monday she died. God told Abraham to kill his son Isaac. He made all the preparation to the point of tying him on the altar with knife in hand. In Genesis 22:12, God stopped him at the last moment:

> *And He said, "Do not stretch out your hand against the lad, and do nothing to him; for now I know that you fear God, since you have not withheld your son, your only son, from Me."*

He was going in one direction with His faith in obedience to God, but was rerouted. I believe that also happened with Nancy. Her faith was definitely proven to God. Despite the progressive deterioration and pain in her body, it never influenced her profession that God is good and true to His Word. She continued to believe for her healing. She lived on pure faith-in and devotion-to Him. I believe God interrupted that faith and said, "You're coming home. You fought the good fight. Your steadfast faith in Me was victorious through every challenge. Well done, My good and faithful servant. Healing on this earth is not a comparable reward for you. Come see My face. See My glory." That was her heart, and I believe He also wanted her there with Him.

> *Precious in the sight of the Lord is the death of His godly ones*—Psalms 116:15

Walter

In His omniscience, God knew the stubborn will of Walter's heart. He was very resistant to Christianity, affirming himself as an atheist. Through his years of rebellion, Ana continued to tell him about Jesus. When stricken with cancer, he vowed that *he* would beat it. His sickness continued for thirteen months. It was the very journey that it took to open his heart to God. There are people who receive salvation, but don't continue in repentance. They willfully walk away from Jesus, embracing a sinful lifestyle. That could have been Walter's path if a healing immediately followed his commitment to the Lord. "I healed myself as vowed. Who needs God?" satan had Walter bound all of his life. He could have easily slipped back, but God didn't allow satan any attempt at deception. In His sovereignty, God had the right to rescue him right in time while his heart was entrusted to Him. God was patient in waiting for that small window of opportunity that Walter's heart would be His. I am grateful that Walter responded to His mercy and grace.

> *The Lord is not slow about His promise, as some count slowness, but is patient toward you, not wishing for any to perish but for all to come to repentance*—2 Peter 3:9

8

The Little Flower in the Garden

Once upon a time, there was a Gardener who wanted a beautiful garden. He selected all of the plants—trees, flowers, hedges—lots of different kinds. After He carefully studied His yard, He planned where each plant would go. He knew exactly what part of the yard's soil was best for the different plants. He knew where the sun would rise and shine on each one. Some plants needed lots of the morning sun. Some needed afternoon sun. Some needed sun all day long. And others just needed a lot more of the shade. Because He knew just how He wanted His garden to look, He placed each plant in its very own place. He had a plan for each one to be beautiful exactly where it was and that it would look beautiful with all the other plants around it.

One day He planted a tiny seed that would become a little flower. He watered it often and watched over it carefully to protect it from anything that would try to hurt or kill it. The days were passing by and He knew that very soon a teeny tiny green speck would start to break her way through the soil. He looked at it every single morning, and the day finally came that He could see a little greenery peering through the soil. It made Him very happy. He loved that little flower-to-be, and had very special plans for her that were different from the plans for the other plants. He knew that she would want exactly what He wanted, too.

She loved her Gardener because He gave her life and promised to meet all her needs. He took perfect care of her. She gave Him much delight and always knew He loved her. She grew bigger and bigger and liked being able to see the wonderful things around her; but more than that, she wanted to be with Him.

As the days, weeks, months, and years passed, the plants were growing and getting more and more beautiful. But there were times when the sun was scorching and blazing hot! The atmosphere would be sweltering, and the plants would sometimes get very, very dry! And there were days when insects would eat their leaves. Then there were storms, too. And at times there were heavy rains, and occasionally hail, that beat on their heads. Cold seasons would come, and some of the plants would fade away until the springtime. Then they would grow again, because their strong deep roots were still alive in the ground. They loved it when they were in full bloom, making the garden a very pleasant place. But the worse days were when the cats used the bathroom on them! That was really stinky and almost destroyed some of the sweet little plants.

Their Gardener was wonderful! He always took the very best care of them through any and every problem. When the sun was scorching hot, He watered them. If the insects tried to hurt them, He sprayed insecticide to kill those bad insects. For all the different diseases, He applied just the right mixture to heal and protect the plants. If they fell over in the storms, He put them back into the ground in a strong upright position; then He pat the soil all around them for sturdy support. But you know what? Those rains and storms also did some good things. Their Gardener knew that, even though the plants did not like the hard rains at the time, they always saw that the storm was good for them after it was all over. They were always more beautiful. Another thing about the long rains was that it made the ground very soft and the Gardener would be able to pull the weeds out much easier. You see, the weeds tried to grow a lot around the plants, and make the garden ugly. Actually, the weeds tried to replace the pretty plants. The Gardener never allowed that to happen. He loved His plants so much.

But, ooooh, the cats! He really had to work hard on them! It was a constant battle, and no matter what, the Gardener was going to make sure that His plants were protected.

The little flower loved her Gardener and was curious about His house. She wondered what it would be like to be with Him there. One day, when He opened the door to go inside, she was able to sneak a little peek. She didn't see much in the short time that the door was open; but what she did see was wonderful, much more so than she could've ever imagined. Everything there was making very holy, beautiful music; and the singing was continuous. As she got a little bigger, she was able to see through the window and into a lot more of the Gardener's house. Wow! She looked all around, from room to room. It was glorious! Everything was so neat and clean. There were always lots and lots of bright sunlight shining directly from the Gardener, and through the windows as well, but no scorching sun. It was cool, restful, and peaceful. No insects were to be seen anywhere! And best of all, there were no CATS! She saw other plants and flowers in different places of the rooms and longed to be there, too. She could tell that they all brought pleasure to the Gardener. She loved to see Him resting there, enjoying the peace and glory of His home. Even though He walked through the garden every day, enjoying His plants outside, this was the place that He lived.

The little flower looked through the window as much as possible. She wanted more and more to be with Him in His majestic home, and said she would do anything to be there. But she knew that He placed her exactly where she was in the garden to please Him. So she remained there happily with all the other plants, obeying Him with all of her little heart. Sometimes the bees took some of her sweetness to make honey with it. She was always willing to give them whatever they needed. She also gave her heart to helping the other plants to do their very best, and they loved her. The Gardener placed her next to a big sago palm and just behind a pretty grass plant. Her bright red color made their deep greens gorgeous! But she never drew any attention to herself. Her only desire was to please the Gardener. And by the way, her contentment to stay in the background made her beauty stand out even more.

The little flower went through some hard times in the garden, and the Gardener always took care of her. She trusted Him with all of her heart and knew that whatever happened there (with insects, scorching sun, et cetera), He would always come at the right time to make things all better. The more He cared for her, the greater her love for Him grew. She gave it everything she had to do her best for Him. And when she made mistakes, He loved her and gave her all the help she needed to reach that goal.

One day the little flower suffered a tragedy, and it looked bad for her. A big ole cat was digging a hole to use the bathroom, and he dug so close to her that his claws pulled her out of the ground, injuring her pretty badly. Her little head was crushed and her leaves were torn. The sun was quickly drying out her unprotected, damaged roots. (For plants to live, they have to always remain in the ground and be watered regularly.) When the Gardener saw how sick and weak she was, He took her to his big shed. He usually just replanted her little plant-being and it would heal. But now He carried out a different plan, the wonderful surprise that He always had for her. But it did not look that way.

When He took her out of the garden, He hung her upside down by a string in the shed. Day after day, she hung in that place without receiving water. She was slowly drying out completely. She knew that she would die if she was not put back into the soil and given water. But she trusted the Gardener, knowing that He always had the answer to mend things. She wanted to return to the garden, to please her Master. The other plants missed her and wanted her back with them very badly. They prayed for her to return to her place in the garden, so that she could live her full life, doing all that the Gardener wanted for her to do there. They loved her so much.

But life was leaving the sweet little flower more and more every day. Her Master was all that she could think about. Just as when He planted her as a tiny seed in the ground and daily checked on her growth and needs, He went to the shed every day to watch over her as she hung from the string. His presence was very comforting, but she expected Him to put her back into the garden at any minute, completely well again. He had done that for her and lots of the other plants before. Her family and friends also had faith, because He promised to always take care of all their needs. They wanted her back with them, doing even greater things than before for the Gardener. They prayed for one of His miracles, and believed with all of their hearts. But they didn't know what He knew.

The little flower barely had any energy left, except just enough to tell the Gardener that she loved Him and that she trusts Him, and that He's good. He saw how the little plant never complained, and how she trusted Him to care perfectly for her as He did in the past. She pleased Him so much that He wanted to give her that very, very special thing that He had always planned for her—the thing that she herself always wanted.

Finally, the day came that there was no more life in the little flower. The other plants were very sad. They loved their Gardener, too. He always did things perfectly for them, and they did not understand why it turned out differently this time.

Then they remembered how the little flower would look into the Master's home as she peered through the window. They also remembered how she really, really wanted to be there so badly. Looking through the window, they could see that everything was so perfect. And there were lots of plants throughout the room, plants that were in the garden at one time. Heavenly, angelic praise and worship music and songs were heard throughout the house. It seemed to be coming from the flowers and the Angels that were there. It was so glorious!

They looked through the window, but as they continued to search and search for the little flower in the different rooms, they could not find her. They knew she was there, and they were happy for her; but they missed her so much. All of a sudden, they heard a voice they knew. It was coming from where their Gardener was, sitting in His favorite chair, enjoying His peaceful home and every song that was being sung to Him. They were praising Him all day long. The familiar voice was joyfully singing from her heart. The plants finally spotted her in the middle of a large beautiful bouquet of dried flowers, and could tell that she was very happy to be with her Master. And you know what? All of the flowers that stayed in His home were made alive again, and they were all so perfect! The little flower's head was now healed and her leaves were no longer torn. They remembered how badly she looked when she was in the shed. Now it looked like she was never hurt at all, and she was more beautiful than she EVER was in the garden! The Gardener was so pleased with how well she served Him there, that He set her right next to His chair in His favorite place. All of the flowers and plants were very happy together forever. There were only happy times and never ever anything bad: no extreme heat or freeze, no insects, no thunder, no diseases, and no storms. Oh! And especially no cats to use the bathroom on her!!

She never knew the Gardener was going to take her home early, instead of leaving her in the garden to serve Him a really long time. You see, even though the little flower loved pleasing the Master in the garden, her original cry was to be in His home with Him in all of His glory. She longed for that for a very long time. But she only knew life as being in the garden and that there was a lot for her to enjoy there with Him, and a lot for her to do for Him.

The Gardener knew that she would be lovely in His home right next to Him, and that she would do whatever it would take for her to get there. But she just did not realize she could get there early in her life on earth. In her time in the shed, hanging by the string, she had a lot of intimate time with just the Master. She spent so much time with Him that her desire for life in the garden was beginning to fade from her heart. After all, she was with the Gardener whom she loved above all else. Now, more than ever, she wanted to be with Him in His home. He whispered in her ear that He was taking her to be with Him a little before she faded out. He wanted to reward her for pleasing Him with a whole heart.

If the little flower was cut and placed in a vase of water in the house, eventually she would have died and been thrown away, IF she did not serve the Gardener. But she did serve Him with a whole heart. Therefore,

He continued His plan for her. The whole time that she hung on the string, her life was being drained and she was being preserved for Him. All she thought about was her Master, and she finally gave up everything to go be with Him forever where there's only happiness. It took her death to make her heart's desire possible.

The Gardener knew, too, that when one flower is picked in a certain way, more than one will come back to replace that one. Also, some flowers have seeds that drop into the ground—and even if the plant is removed—its seeds will still grow new plants like them. God does this in people, by passing Nanu's talents on to us, so that we will be stronger than before for Him. Our faith pleased Him, and He also will do something special in us, but it will be different.

Lacey, Kaitlyn, Eric, Micah, thank you for praying for Nanu. She wanted very much to see Jesus' glory, and has always wanted to be with Him. But she did not know that God had a very high place especially for her in Heaven. Sometimes when someone has great faith in God during very painful times, He searches their heart to see what their biggest desire is and wants to reward them with that very special reward. For Nanu that was to see His face and glory. She faithfully confessed that He's a good God, no matter how bad things were. She believed for her healing, always saying that His Word is true. Never did she ever complain or become angry. She honored and pleased Him so much with her faith, that He said, "Healing on this earth is not enough of a reward for you. Back in 1982 you said that you wanted to see My glory. You cried out to see My face. You've been faithful and always believed My Word." Then He reached down, took her into His cupped hands, and carried her straight up to Heaven. Holding her before His face, He said, "See My face and see My glory." Her faith did far more than a wonderful miracle of healing. It took her to a high place in Heaven, where she really saw all of His glory! It made her very, very happy and that's forever! Nanu will never ever suffer again.

Thank y'all for faithfully praying for Nanu with all of your hearts. You see, she could not have persevered all alone. She desperately needed everyone's prayers to help keep her strong. God will reward each of you for your prayers and encouragement when y'all get to Heaven—and you know what? If it were any sort of a crown, I wonder if Jesus just might be letting Nanu hold on to them in her mansion, waiting for you all to come up there, so that she herself might have the privilege of putting them on your heads for Him? (Really, I think that Jesus would want to do that!)

Afterword

No matter how dedicated and strong a Christian you are (and if not a Christian at all), please read this. After forty years of being a very focused Christian and continually going forward in my walk, my eyes were opened to truths that I missed. Please...study these Scriptures in context and search the Word. They're not isolated verses. They have many cross references.

1. Luke 10:25–28 *You shall love the Lord your God with all your heart, and with all your soul, and with all your strength, and with all your mind; and your neighbor as yourself* —This was the answer given when a lawyer asked how to obtain eternal life. Some of our wrong ways and attitudes may seem minor to us, but we can't hold back any part of our hearts. Please be careful. (Jesus says in John 14:15, "If you love Me, you will keep My commandments." To love Him means to obey Him.)

2. Galatians 5:19–21 *Now the deeds of the flesh are evident, which are: immorality, impurity, sensuality, (20) idolatry,*

sorcery, enmities, strife, jealousy, outbursts of anger, dis-putes, dissensions, factions, (21) envying, drunkenness, carousing, and things like these, of which I forewarn you just as I have forewarned you that those who practice such things shall not inherit the kingdom of God.—These practices are very common to Christians. God loves us so much and wants us to spend eternity with Him. The Holy Spirit will show us ways from which we need to turn and will help us to overcome them.

3. Mark 13:13...*but the one who endures to the end, he shall be saved.*—God is very merciful when we falter. He also gives us His abundant grace to be overcomers, so that we can endure. Jesus did all the work of defeating satan and we can live out our salvation with His help through grace. It is a continual life long process.

4. Mattthew 7:14 *"For the gate is small, and the way is narrow that leads to life, and few are those who find it."*— Ask Jesus to come into your life right now, repent of sin, and read your Bible daily. Let Him change you into His image, so that you can be ready when He comes back for His people, or at the time of your death. Only Jesus can live the Christian life. Allow Him live it through you. We have to let Him be Lord in every sense of the word.